# Reflections of the Mind

## Exploring Philosophy's Depths

Shantanu S. Khandare

ISBN 978-93-5883-051-4
© Shantanu S. Khandare 2023

Published in India 2023 by Pencil

*A brand of*
One Point Six Technologies Pvt. Ltd.
Unit no. 26, Ground Floor, Building A1,
Wadala Truck Terminal Road,
Near Post Office, Antop Hill, Mumbai - 400037
**E** connect@thepencilapp.com
**W** www.thepencilapp.com



DISCLAIMER: *The opinions expressed in this book are those of the authors and do not purport to reflect the views of the Publisher.*

# Author biography

Shantanu Khandare is a prolific social life motivator and blogger, making a significant impact since 2018. Through his insightful and inspiring blog articles, he has been helping individuals navigate through life's challenges and discover the keys to living a fulfilling existence.

Shantanu's expertise lies in addressing various life problems, offering practical advice, and motivating readers to embrace a positive mindset. With his engaging writing style and deep understanding of human nature, he has become a trusted source of guidance for those seeking personal growth and happiness. Shantanu Khandare's profound impact as a professional blogger is a testament to his passion for empowering others and making a difference in their lives.

# CONTENTS

# About Book

"Reflections of the Mind: Exploring Philosophy's Depths" takes readers on a captivating journey through the vast landscape of philosophy. From the timeless questions about the nature of reality, knowledge, and morality to the pressing issues of our modern world, this book offers thought-provoking insights into the fundamental aspects of human existence.

In this comprehensive and engaging exploration of philosophy, we delve into various branches of philosophical inquiry, including metaphysics, epistemology, ethics, political philosophy, aesthetics, existentialism, feminist philosophy, and environmental philosophy. Each chapter delves into the depths of its respective field, presenting key concepts, theories, and perspectives that have shaped philosophical discourse throughout history and continue to shape our understanding of the world today.

The book is organized into fifteen chapters, with each chapter focusing on a specific branch of philosophy. From the profound questions of metaphysics that probe the nature of reality and existence, to the ethical dilemmas that challenge our moral compass, to the exploration of the human condition in existentialism, each chapter offers an in-depth examination of its subject matter. Additionally, chapters on feminist philosophy and environmental philosophy provide crucial insights into pressing social and environmental issues, highlighting the importance of justice, equality, and our interconnectedness with the natural world.

Within each chapter, readers will find detailed analyses, engaging discussions, and thought-provoking questions that encourage introspection and critical thinking. The chapters are structured to provide a comprehensive understanding of the central concepts, theories, and debates within each branch of philosophy, making the book accessible to both beginners and those familiar with philosophical discourse.

As readers embark on this philosophical journey, they will be challenged to examine their own beliefs, assumptions, and values. Through the exploration of diverse perspectives and theories, "Reflections of the Mind" encourages readers to engage with philosophy as a means of expanding their intellectual horizons, enhancing their understanding of the human experience, and fostering a deeper appreciation for the complexities of the world in which we live.

With its comprehensive scope and accessible style, "Reflections of the Mind: Exploring Philosophy's Depths" serves as a valuable resource for students, philosophers, and anyone interested in exploring the profound questions that captivate human thought. It invites readers to embark on an intellectual adventure, guiding them through the depths of philosophy and inspiring them to reflect on their own place in the intricate tapestry of existence.

Whether you are a novice seeking an introduction to philosophy or a seasoned philosopher seeking new perspectives, "Reflections of the Mind" offers an enlightening and thought-provoking journey that will deepen your understanding of philosophy and its profound impact on human thought and existence. Open your mind, challenge your assumptions, and embark on this philosophical exploration that will leave you with a richer and more nuanced understanding of the world and your place within it.

# Message for Reader's

Dear Readers,

Welcome to "Reflections of the Mind: Exploring Philosophy's Depths." As you embark on this philosophical journey, we invite you to open your mind, question your assumptions, and delve into the profound questions that have captivated human thought throughout history.

Philosophy offers a unique lens through which we can examine the complexities of existence, the nature of reality, the foundations of knowledge, and the moral principles that guide our actions. It challenges us to explore our place in the world and grapple with the profound questions that shape our lives.

In this book, you will encounter a diverse range of philosophical perspectives, from ancient wisdom to contemporary debates. Each chapter delves into a specific branch of philosophy, providing a comprehensive exploration of its key concepts, theories, and implications. Whether you are a seasoned philosopher or new to the world of philosophical inquiry, we aim to make this journey accessible and thought-provoking.

We encourage you to approach each chapter with an open and inquisitive mind. Engage with the ideas presented, question their implications, and reflect on how they resonate with your own beliefs and experiences. Philosophy is not meant to provide all the answers but rather to spark deep reflection and inspire intellectual growth.

Throughout this book, you will encounter diverse perspectives, challenging debates, and profound insights. We invite you to embrace the richness of these perspectives and engage in thoughtful dialogue. Philosophy thrives on discussion and the exchange of ideas, so feel free to share your thoughts, engage in conversations, and seek to deepen your understanding through interaction with others.

As you navigate the pages of "Reflections of the Mind," we hope you will find inspiration, intellectual stimulation, and a renewed appreciation for the profound questions that lie at the heart of human existence. Philosophy invites us to explore the depths of our minds, to question, to seek meaning, and to challenge the status quo.

Ultimately, we hope this book encourages you to embark on your own philosophical journey. Allow these reflections to serve as a starting point, igniting a lifelong pursuit of knowledge, wisdom, and a deeper understanding of yourself and the world around you.

Thank you for joining us on this intellectual adventure. May "Reflections of the Mind: Exploring Philosophy's

Depths" broaden your horizons, deepen your insights, and inspire you to engage with the profound questions that captivate human thought.

Sincerely,
Shantanu S. Khandare

# Introduction of Book

In a world filled with complexities, uncertainties, and profound questions, philosophy emerges as a guiding light, inviting us to embark on a journey of intellectual exploration and self-discovery. It is within the realm of philosophy that we grapple with fundamental inquiries about the nature of reality, the limits of knowledge, the nature of morality, and the purpose of our existence. "Reflections of the Mind: Exploring Philosophy's Depths" is a book that aims to illuminate this journey, guiding readers through the vast expanse of human thought and inviting them to delve into the profound depths of philosophy.

In this captivating exploration, we embark on a multidimensional exploration of philosophy's branches and concepts. From the ancient wisdom of thinkers such as Socrates, Plato, and Aristotle to the groundbreaking ideas of contemporary philosophers, this book presents a tapestry of philosophical perspectives that have shaped and continue to shape our understanding of the world.

"Reflections of the Mind" is organized into chapters that explore various branches of philosophy, such as metaphysics, epistemology, ethics, political philosophy, aesthetics, existentialism, feminist philosophy, and environmental philosophy. Each chapter delves into the depths of its respective field, unraveling the intricacies of philosophical discourse and presenting key concepts, theories, and perspectives.

Throughout this journey, readers will encounter profound questions that transcend time and space. We confront the nature of reality, contemplating the existence of universals, the mind-body problem, and the limits of human knowledge. We explore ethical dilemmas, reflecting on the foundations of morality, the nature of moral responsibility, and the quest for justice. We delve into political philosophy, considering questions of power, governance, and the social contract. We examine aesthetics, contemplating the nature of beauty, the role of art, and the subjective experience of aesthetic appreciation. We confront existential angst, embracing the complexities of human existence, freedom, and the search for meaning. We engage with feminist philosophy, challenging patriarchal norms and advocating for gender equality. And we explore environmental philosophy, contemplating our ethical responsibilities towards the natural world and our interconnectedness with it.

As we journey through the pages of "Reflections of the Mind," we are invited to engage actively with the material, to question our assumptions, and to critically evaluate the ideas presented. Philosophy is not a passive endeavor; it requires active participation and intellectual curiosity. By delving into the depths of philosophical inquiry, we cultivate critical thinking skills, expand our intellectual horizons, and develop a deeper understanding of ourselves and the world in which we live.

"Reflections of the Mind" is intended for both newcomers to philosophy and seasoned thinkers. It is a book that invites readers to embark on an intellectual adventure, fostering a sense of wonder, curiosity, and awe for the profound questions that lie at the heart of human thought. Through engaging narratives, accessible explanations, and thought-provoking questions, this book aims to make philosophy accessible and relevant to our lives.

As you delve into the pages of "Reflections of the Mind: Exploring Philosophy's Depths," I encourage you to approach each chapter with an open mind and a willingness to explore the depths of human thought. Embrace the challenges and uncertainties that philosophical inquiry presents, and allow yourself to be transformed by the ideas and insights that emerge from this journey.

May "Reflections of the Mind" ignite a spark within you— a spark of intellectual curiosity, a thirst for wisdom, and a profound appreciation for the depth and complexity of the philosophical exploration that awaits. Enjoy the journey, embrace the reflections, and may your mind be forever enriched by the exploration of philosophy's profound depths.

# Chapter 1 The Origins of Philosophical Inquiry

**Introduction**:

The quest for wisdom and understanding has been an enduring feature of human civilization. From the earliest moments of self-awareness, individuals have grappled with fundamental questions about the nature of reality, the purpose of life, and the existence of the divine. This chapter takes us back to the origins of philosophical inquiry, tracing its roots to ancient civilizations and exploring the intellectual pioneers who laid the groundwork for centuries of philosophical exploration.

1.1 The Dawn of Philosophical Thought:

In the ancient world, philosophy emerged as a distinct discipline, breaking away from myth, religion, and folklore. The city of Miletus in Ancient Greece witnessed the birth of the first philosophers known as the Milesian School, with Thales, Anaximander, and Anaximenes at its helm. These thinkers sought to explain the world through naturalistic explanations, moving away from supernatural narratives.

1.2 The Legacy of Pre-Socratic Thinkers:

The Pre-Socratic philosophers, such as Heraclitus,

Parmenides, and Democritus, expanded upon the Milesian School's ideas and developed their own theories. Heraclitus proposed that the fundamental nature of reality is in a constant state of flux, famously stating that "you cannot step into the same river twice." Parmenides, on the other hand, argued for the existence of a stable and unchanging reality, asserting that change is an illusion. Democritus put forth the concept of atomism, suggesting that all matter is composed of indivisible particles called atoms.

1.3 Socrates and the Socratic Method:
Socrates, an iconic figure in the history of philosophy, shifted the focus from cosmology to ethics and human nature. He believed that the pursuit of knowledge was intimately connected with moral virtue and the examination of one's own beliefs. Through his Socratic method of questioning, he encouraged individuals to critically reflect on their assumptions and engage in rational dialogue to arrive at a deeper understanding.

1.4 Plato and the Theory of Forms:
Plato, Socrates' most famous student, founded the Academy and developed a comprehensive philosophical system. He posited the existence of an eternal realm of Forms or Ideas, which he considered to be the true reality behind the imperfect and ever-changing world of appearances. Plato's writings, including his famous work "The Republic," delve into topics such as justice, knowledge, and the nature of the soul.

1.5 Aristotle and the Pursuit of Wisdom:
Aristotle, Plato's student at the Academy, embarked on a philosophical journey that spanned numerous disciplines. His comprehensive approach to knowledge influenced fields ranging from biology to logic. Aristotle's philosophical system emphasized the study of nature and the empirical observation of the physical world. He classified different branches of knowledge, delved into ethics, and proposed his famous principle of the golden mean, advocating for moderation and balance in all aspects of life.

1.6 Philosophical Traditions Beyond Greece:
While ancient Greece witnessed a remarkable flourishing of philosophical thought, other civilizations also contributed to the development of philosophical ideas. The Indian subcontinent gave rise to various schools of thought, including the Vedanta, Nyaya, and Samkhya schools. Chinese philosophy, with its emphasis on Confucianism, Daoism, and Legalism, offered unique perspectives on ethics, governance, and the nature of reality.

Conclusion:
The origins of philosophical inquiry can be traced back to the ancient world, where thinkers from diverse cultures embarked on a quest for knowledge, wisdom, and understanding. From the early Milesian philosophers to the profound insights of Socrates, Plato, and Aristotle, these intellectual pioneers laid the groundwork for centuries of philosophical exploration. Their ideas continue to shape our understanding of the world and ourselves, inviting us

to engage in critical reflection, questioning, and the pursuit of truth. In the following chapters, we will delve further into the rich tapestry of philosophical thought, exploring its various branches and examining the enduring questions that continue to captivate human minds.

# Chapter 2 The Ancient Greek Philosophers From Socrates to Aristotle

Introduction:

The ancient Greek philosophers have left an indelible mark on the history of philosophical thought. From Socrates' emphasis on self-examination and moral virtue to Plato's exploration of metaphysics and Aristotle's systematic approach to knowledge, these thinkers laid the foundation for Western philosophy. In this chapter, we delve into the lives, ideas, and legacies of some of the most influential ancient Greek philosophers.

## 2.1 Socrates: The Examined Life

Socrates, often hailed as the father of Western philosophy, dedicated his life to the pursuit of wisdom and virtue. Unlike his predecessors, he focused on ethics and the examination of one's beliefs through the Socratic method of questioning. Socrates believed that true knowledge could be attained by challenging assumptions and engaging in rational dialogue. His unwavering commitment to truth ultimately led to his trial and execution, leaving a profound legacy that continues to inspire philosophical inquiry to this day.

## 2.2 Plato: The Realm of Forms

Plato, a student of Socrates, established the Academy and developed a philosophical system that would shape Western thought for centuries. He believed in the existence of a transcendent realm of Forms or Ideas, which he considered to be the true reality behind the imperfect world of appearances. Plato's metaphysics, as expounded in dialogues such as "The Republic" and "The Symposium," explored the nature of knowledge, justice, and the human soul. His concept of an ideal society governed by philosopher-kings continues to provoke discussions on governance and the pursuit of the good life.

## 2.3 Aristotle: The Pursuit of Knowledge

Aristotle, a student of Plato, ventured beyond the confines of metaphysics to encompass a wide range of subjects, including biology, physics, logic, and ethics. His systematic approach to knowledge laid the groundwork for the development of the scientific method. Aristotle categorized different branches of knowledge, investigating the nature of causality and advocating for empirical observation. His ethical theory centered around the cultivation of virtues and the pursuit of eudaimonia, or flourishing. Aristotle's works, such as "Nicomachean Ethics" and "Physics," remain foundational texts in philosophy and science.

## 2.4 Hellenistic Philosophies: Stoicism, Epicureanism, and Skepticism

In the wake of Aristotle's teachings, Hellenistic philosophy flourished, giving rise to diverse schools of thought. Stoicism, founded by Zeno of Citium, emphasized the pursuit of virtue, inner tranquility, and acceptance of one's fate. Epicureanism, influenced by Epicurus, advocated for a life of pleasure understood as tranquility and freedom from unnecessary desires. Skepticism, championed by philosophers such as Pyrrho of Elis, encouraged the suspension of judgment and the recognition of the limits of human knowledge.

2.5 The Influence of Ancient Greek Philosophy

The philosophical ideas of ancient Greece permeated subsequent intellectual traditions, leaving a lasting impact on Western civilization. The works of Socrates, Plato, and Aristotle were preserved and studied throughout the Middle Ages and the Renaissance, fueling the development of philosophical, scientific, and political thought. Their emphasis on rational inquiry, moral reflection, and the pursuit of truth continues to shape contemporary philosophical discourse.

Conclusion:

The ancient Greek philosophers, from Socrates to Aristotle, revolutionized the landscape of philosophical thought. Socrates' commitment to self-examination and ethical inquiry set the stage for a more introspective and reflective approach to philosophy. Plato's exploration of metaphysics and his concept of the Forms expanded the boundaries of human knowledge, while Aristotle's systematic approach to understanding the natural world and ethical principles laid the foundation for scientific inquiry and ethical theory. The legacy of these thinkers extends far beyond their time, influencing subsequent generations of philosophers and shaping the intellectual landscape of Western civilization. In the following chapters, we will continue to explore the vast terrain of philosophy, building upon the ideas and insights forged by these ancient Greek masters.

# Chapter 3 The Eastern Philosophical Traditions Buddhism, Taoism, and Confucianism

Introduction:

While ancient Greek philosophy has often taken center stage in Western intellectual history, the Eastern philosophical traditions offer profound insights into the nature of existence, morality, and the human condition. In this chapter, we explore three prominent Eastern philosophical traditions: Buddhism, Taoism, and Confucianism. Each of these traditions presents a unique perspective on life, ethics, and the quest for enlightenment.

3.1 Buddhism: The Path to Enlightenment

Buddhism, founded by Siddhartha Gautama, also known as the Buddha, emerged in ancient India and has since spread across various parts of Asia. Central to Buddhist philosophy is the recognition of suffering as an inherent part of existence. The Four Noble Truths, elucidated by the Buddha, emphasize the nature of suffering, its causes, and the possibility of its cessation through the Eightfold Path. Buddhist teachings delve into the impermanence of all things, the interconnectedness of life, and the practice of mindfulness and compassion. The goal of Buddhism is to attain enlightenment and liberation from the cycle of rebirth.

3.2 Taoism: Harmony with the Way

Taoism, originating in ancient China, centers around the concept of the Tao, which can be understood as the underlying principle of the universe. The Tao is characterized by spontaneity, harmony, and balance. Taoist philosophy emphasizes the cultivation of wu-wei, or non-action, which does not imply inactivity but rather aligning oneself with the natural flow of existence. The writings of Laozi, the foundational text "Tao Te Ching," and the teachings of Zhuangzi expound upon the wisdom of embracing simplicity, naturalness, and humility. Taoism encourages individuals to harmonize with the rhythms of nature and to seek inner tranquility.

3.3 Confucianism: Moral Governance and Social Harmony

Confucianism, developed by Confucius and his followers, shaped the ethical and social framework of ancient China and continues to influence East Asian cultures today. Confucian philosophy centers on the cultivation of virtues, such as benevolence, righteousness, and filial piety. It emphasizes the importance of social harmony, ethical conduct, and the pursuit of moral excellence. Confucian teachings underscore the significance of proper relationships, ethical governance, and the realization of the junzi, or the morally exemplary person. The Analects, a collection of Confucius' sayings and teachings, expounds upon the principles of Confucian ethics and the ideal of a just society.

## 3.4 Interconnections and Diverse Perspectives

While Buddhism, Taoism, and Confucianism each represent distinct philosophical traditions, they are not mutually exclusive. Throughout history, these traditions have often interacted, influenced one another, and coexisted within the same cultural milieu. The concept of emptiness in Buddhism finds resonance in the Taoist notion of the void, while Confucianism incorporates elements of both Buddhism and Taoism in its ethical framework. The interconnectedness and fluidity of these traditions contribute to a vibrant and dynamic philosophical landscape in the East.

## 3.5 Impact and Global Relevance

The Eastern philosophical traditions have transcended their original cultural contexts and gained global recognition and relevance. Their teachings offer valuable insights into the nature of human existence, the pursuit of wisdom, and the cultivation of moral character. The practices of mindfulness, meditation, and ethical conduct advocated by Buddhism have found resonance in contemporary Western societies. Taoist principles of simplicity, harmony, and naturalness have inspired individuals seeking a more balanced and fulfilling way of life. Confucian ethics, with its emphasis on social harmony and moral governance, has influenced discussions on ethics, education, and social relationships.

## Conclusion:

The Eastern philosophical traditions of Buddhism, Taoism, and Confucianism provide profound wisdom and unique perspectives on life, ethics, and the nature of reality. Buddhism's emphasis on enlightenment and compassion, Taoism's embrace of natural harmony, and Confucianism's focus on moral governance and social harmony offer diverse paths for individuals seeking understanding and personal growth. The interconnections and dynamic nature of these traditions reflect the richness and complexity of Eastern thought. By exploring these traditions, we expand our philosophical horizons and gain new insights into the human experience. In the following chapters, we will continue our philosophical journey, drawing upon the wisdom of both Western and Eastern traditions to deepen our understanding of the fundamental questions of existence.

# Chapter 4 Rationalism vs. Empiricism Debating the Sources of Knowledge

Introduction:

The question of how knowledge is acquired and what constitutes a reliable source of knowledge has been a central concern in philosophy for centuries. In this chapter, we delve into the debate between rationalism and empiricism, two prominent philosophical schools of thought that propose contrasting views on the sources, nature, and limits of human knowledge. By exploring the arguments and insights of rationalists and empiricists, we aim to gain a deeper understanding of the complex nature of knowledge acquisition.

## 4.1 Rationalism: Knowledge Through Reason

Rationalism asserts that reason and innate mental capacities are the primary sources of knowledge. Rationalists argue that certain fundamental truths and principles can be grasped through pure reason, independent of sensory experience. René Descartes, a prominent rationalist, famously declared, "I think, therefore I am," affirming the existence of the self as a foundational truth derived from introspection and logical analysis. Rationalists also emphasize the role of deductive reasoning in deriving new knowledge from these foundational truths. Other notable rationalist philosophers include Gottfried Wilhelm Leibniz and Baruch Spinoza, who sought to establish a systematic framework for understanding reality through logical and mathematical principles.

4.2 Empiricism: Knowledge Through Experience

Empiricism, in contrast to rationalism, argues that all knowledge is derived from sensory experience. Empiricists maintain that the mind is a blank slate, or tabula rasa, at birth, and that knowledge is acquired through perception, observation, and experimentation. John Locke, a prominent empiricist, proposed the theory of simple and complex ideas, suggesting that all knowledge is ultimately derived from sensory impressions. David Hume, another influential empiricist, emphasized the importance of empirical evidence and causality in understanding the world. Empiricism places great emphasis on the scientific method and the accumulation of empirical data to validate or reject hypotheses.

4.3 The Debate and the Problem of Innate Ideas

The debate between rationalism and empiricism revolves around the question of whether there are innate ideas or concepts that exist independently of sensory experience. Rationalists argue that certain knowledge, such as mathematical truths or the concept of God, is inherently present in the mind from birth. Empiricists, however, contend that all knowledge is acquired through sensory experience and that there are no innate ideas. This debate raises philosophical challenges regarding the nature of perception, the reliability of sense data, and the role of language in shaping our understanding of the world.

## 4.4 Reconciliation and Synthesis

While rationalism and empiricism have historically been presented as opposing viewpoints, many philosophers have sought to reconcile or synthesize elements of both perspectives. Immanuel Kant, for example, proposed a transcendental synthesis, arguing that while knowledge is derived from experience, the mind actively structures and organizes sensory data according to innate cognitive categories. This synthesis allows for the recognition of the importance of both reason and experience in the acquisition of knowledge.

## 4.5 Contemporary Perspectives and Extensions

The rationalism-empiricism debate continues to resonate in contemporary philosophy, with various perspectives contributing to the ongoing discussion. Cognitive science, for instance, examines the interplay between cognitive processes, neural mechanisms, and the acquisition of knowledge. Pragmatism, another philosophical approach, focuses on the practical consequences and usefulness of beliefs rather than their theoretical foundations. These and other contemporary perspectives contribute to a nuanced understanding of the complex relationship between reason, experience, and knowledge.

## Conclusion:

The debate between rationalism and empiricism offers valuable insights into the sources and nature of human knowledge. While rationalists emphasize the role of reason and innate mental capacities, empiricists stress the significance of sensory experience and empirical evidence. The exploration of this debate raises fundamental questions about the reliability of different sources of knowledge, the problem of innate ideas, and the role of language and perception in shaping our understanding of the world. As we delve further into the realm of philosophy, we will encounter diverse perspectives that build upon and challenge the rationalism-empiricism framework, broadening our understanding of knowledge acquisition and the complexities of human cognition.

# Chapter 5 The Nature of Reality
## Metaphysics and Ontology

Introduction:
Metaphysics and ontology are branches of philosophy concerned with the fundamental nature of reality, existence, and being. In this chapter, we embark on a philosophical exploration of the nature of reality, delving into questions about the ultimate structure of the universe, the nature of existence, and the fundamental properties of reality itself. Through the lenses of metaphysics and ontology, we seek to unravel the mysteries that lie at the heart of our understanding of the world.

5.1 Metaphysics: The Study of Ultimate Reality
Metaphysics is the branch of philosophy that examines the nature of reality beyond the physical realm. It delves into questions of existence, identity, causality, and the relationship between mind and matter. Metaphysical inquiries explore the fundamental principles that govern the world and seek to uncover the underlying structure of reality. Ancient philosophers such as Parmenides, who argued for the existence of a single unchanging reality, and Heraclitus, who emphasized the ever-changing nature of existence, paved the way for metaphysical inquiry.

5.2 Ontology: The Study of Being
Ontology focuses specifically on the study of being and existence. It seeks to understand the categories of existence and the nature of entities that populate the world. Ontological investigations examine questions about the nature of objects, properties, relations, and the distinctions between different types of beings. Ontologists explore concepts such as substance, causality, identity, and the nature of time and space. The works of philosophers such as Aristotle, who proposed categories of being, and Martin Heidegger, who delved into the nature of being-in-the-world, have greatly influenced ontological thought.

5.3 Realism: The External World and Independent Reality
Realism, within metaphysics and ontology, posits the existence of an external world that exists independently of human perception or cognition. Realists argue that reality has objective properties and structures that exist regardless of our subjective experience or interpretation. Philosophers like Plato advocated for a form of metaphysical realism, positing the existence of abstract, ideal Forms that serve as the true reality behind the perceived world of appearances. In contemporary philosophy, scientific realism extends this perspective by asserting that scientific theories aim to provide an accurate description of the external world.

5.4 Idealism: The Primacy of Consciousness and Ideas
Idealism, in contrast to realism, holds that reality is fundamentally mental or dependent on consciousness. Idealists argue that the external world is inseparable from our subjective experiences and interpretations.

Philosophers such as George Berkeley proposed subjective idealism, suggesting that objects exist only as ideas in the minds of perceivers. Immanuel Kant's transcendental idealism posited that the mind actively structures sensory experience, shaping our understanding of the world. Idealism challenges the notion of an independent external reality and highlights the role of consciousness in shaping our perception of the world.

## 5.5 Dualism: The Mind-Body Problem

The mind-body problem, a significant topic within metaphysics, addresses the relationship between the mind and the body. Dualism posits that the mind and the body are distinct entities with different properties. René Descartes famously proposed substance dualism, arguing that the mind or soul is an immaterial substance separate from the physical body. This view raises questions about the interaction between mind and matter and the nature of consciousness. Alternative perspectives, such as materialism, argue that the mind can be reduced to physical processes in the brain.

## 5.6 Monism: Unity and Fundamental Oneness

Monism proposes that reality is fundamentally one and that all seemingly separate entities or phenomena can be ultimately reduced to a single substance or principle. Monistic perspectives include substance monism, such as Spinoza's pantheism, which posits that everything in the universe is an expression of a single divine substance. Process monism, as proposed by Alfred North Whitehead, suggests that reality consists of dynamic processes rather than fixed substances. Monism challenges dualistic views and seeks to uncover the underlying unity of all existence.

Conclusion:
Metaphysics and ontology offer profound insights into the nature of reality and the fundamental questions of existence. Through metaphysical inquiries, we explore the underlying structure of reality beyond the physical realm, contemplating questions of identity, causality, and the mind-body relationship. Ontology delves into the study of being, examining the categories of existence and the nature of entities that populate the world. Perspectives such as realism emphasize the independent existence of an external world, while idealism highlights the role of consciousness in shaping our understanding of reality. The mind-body problem and the exploration of monistic perspectives further enrich our understanding of the complex nature of existence. By engaging with these philosophical inquiries, we deepen our comprehension of the fundamental nature of reality and our place within it. In the following chapters, we will continue our philosophical journey, exploring additional branches of philosophy and delving further into the mysteries of human existence.

# Chapter 6 Ethics and Morality Navigating the Landscape of Right and Wrong

Introduction:

Ethics and morality are branches of philosophy that deal with questions of right and wrong, good and bad, and the principles that guide human behavior. In this chapter, we embark on an exploration of ethical theories, moral dilemmas, and the quest for moral truth. By examining various perspectives within ethics and morality, we aim to navigate the complex landscape of human values and ethical decision-making.

6.1 Normative Ethics: The Study of Moral Principles

Normative ethics seeks to establish the standards by which we determine what is morally right or wrong. It examines the fundamental principles and rules that guide human behavior and evaluate the morality of actions. Ethical theories within normative ethics provide frameworks for making moral judgments. These theories include consequentialism, deontology, virtue ethics, and ethical relativism, each offering unique perspectives on ethical decision-making.

## 6.2 Consequentialism: The Ethics of Outcomes

Consequentialist theories, such as utilitarianism, focus on the consequences of actions in determining their morality. According to utilitarianism, the right action is the one that maximizes overall happiness or utility for the greatest number of people. Consequentialist approaches emphasize the importance of weighing the potential outcomes and considering the net benefits or harms resulting from different choices.

## 6.3 Deontology: The Ethics of Duties and Principles

Deontological theories, championed by philosophers like Immanuel Kant, emphasize the inherent moral worth of actions themselves, independent of their consequences. Deontologists argue that moral duties and principles should guide ethical decision-making. Kant's categorical imperative, for example, asserts that individuals should act in a way that their actions can be universalized and treated as moral laws.

## 6.4 Virtue Ethics: The Ethics of Character

Virtue ethics focuses on the cultivation of moral character and the development of virtues that lead to ethical behavior. Philosophers like Aristotle emphasize the importance of cultivating virtues such as courage, justice, and wisdom to guide actions. Virtue ethics emphasizes the moral qualities of individuals rather than focusing solely on the morality of specific actions.

## 6.5 Ethical Relativism: Cultural and Subjective Perspectives

Ethical relativism argues that moral judgments are relative to cultural norms, individual beliefs, or personal preferences. It suggests that what is considered morally right or wrong varies across different cultures or individuals. Ethical relativism challenges the existence of universal moral truths and highlights the importance of understanding diverse ethical perspectives.

## 6.6 Moral Dilemmas and Ethical Decision-Making

Moral dilemmas present situations in which there are conflicting moral principles or choices, making it challenging to determine the right course of action. Ethical decision-making involves weighing different ethical theories, considering the consequences, evaluating duties and principles, and reflecting on one's own moral values. It requires careful reasoning and ethical judgment in navigating complex ethical quandaries.

## 6.7 Applied Ethics: Real-World Moral Issues

Applied ethics applies ethical theories and principles to real-world moral issues such as bioethics, environmental ethics, business ethics, and social justice. These fields explore the moral implications of practices and policies and seek to address ethical challenges in specific domains of human activity. Applied ethics involves grappling with issues such as euthanasia, genetic engineering, climate change, corporate responsibility, and inequality.

## Conclusion:

Ethics and morality provide frameworks for understanding and navigating the complex landscape of right and wrong, good and bad. Normative ethics offers different theories and approaches to ethical decision-making, including consequentialism, deontology, virtue ethics, and ethical relativism. Each perspective provides insights into the principles that guide human behavior and the evaluation of moral actions. Moral dilemmas challenge us to critically reflect on conflicting moral principles and make ethically sound choices. Applied ethics extends these theoretical frameworks to address real-world moral issues and guide ethical practices in various domains. By engaging in the study of ethics and morality, we strive to navigate the intricate landscape of human values, ethical decision-making, and the quest for a more just and virtuous society. In the following chapters, we will continue to explore the diverse terrain of philosophy, examining other branches and dimensions of human thought.

# Chapter 7 Epistemology Understanding the Theory of Knowledge

Introduction:

Epistemology is the branch of philosophy that investigates the nature, sources, and limits of knowledge. It explores questions such as: What can we know? How do we acquire knowledge? What are the criteria for justified belief? In this chapter, we delve into the realm of epistemology, examining various theories and perspectives on the theory of knowledge and the process of knowing.

7.1 The Nature of Knowledge:

Epistemology begins by examining the nature of knowledge itself. Knowledge is typically defined as justified true belief. To possess knowledge, one must have a belief that is true and justified by good reasons or evidence. This understanding forms the foundation for exploring the nature and conditions of knowledge.

7.2 Rationalism and Empiricism:

Epistemology encompasses the historical debate between rationalism and empiricism, which we previously encountered in the discussion of sources of knowledge. Rationalism emphasizes the role of reason and innate ideas in acquiring knowledge, while empiricism posits that knowledge is derived from sensory experience. The rationalism-empiricism debate raises questions about the relationship between reason and experience in the acquisition of knowledge.

7.3 Foundationalism and Coherentism:
Foundationalism and coherentism are two competing theories regarding the structure of knowledge. Foundationalism suggests that knowledge is built upon a foundation of basic, self-evident beliefs or incorrigible experiences. These foundational beliefs serve as the starting point for constructing justified beliefs. Coherentism, on the other hand, argues that knowledge is a coherent system of beliefs, with each belief supported by its relation to other beliefs within a broader network of coherence. Coherentism emphasizes the interdependence of beliefs rather than relying on foundational elements.

7.4 Skepticism and the Problem of Justification:
Skepticism challenges our confidence in knowledge by raising doubts about the possibility of attaining justified beliefs. Skeptics argue that we lack sufficient grounds to claim knowledge with certainty. They highlight potential problems of induction, the limitations of perception, and the problem of the external world. Epistemology engages with skepticism to explore the nature of justification, the reliability of evidence, and the boundaries of human knowledge.

7.5 Epistemic Justification and Reliability:
Epistemic justification addresses the question of what constitutes sufficient grounds for claiming knowledge.

Different theories propose criteria for justification, such as foundational beliefs, coherence, empirical evidence, or reliable processes of belief formation. Reliabilism, for instance, argues that beliefs are justified if they are produced by reliable cognitive processes, such as perception, memory, or logical reasoning.

7.6 Epistemic Contextualism and Relativism:
Epistemic contextualism and relativism offer alternative perspectives on knowledge. Contextualism suggests that the truth conditions and standards of knowledge can vary depending on the context in which knowledge claims are made. Relativism takes this idea further, arguing that truth and knowledge are relative to particular cultural, social, or linguistic frameworks. These perspectives challenge the universality and objectivity of knowledge.

7.7 Social Epistemology and the Community of Knowers:
Social epistemology expands the scope of epistemology to include the social and collective dimensions of knowledge. It explores how knowledge is shaped and transmitted through social processes, such as testimony, consensus-building, and communal inquiry. Social epistemology investigates questions of trust, authority, and the influence of social factors on knowledge formation.

Conclusion:
Epistemology investigates the nature, sources, and limits of knowledge, addressing fundamental questions about what we can know and how we acquire knowledge. The debate between rationalism and empiricism, the exploration of foundationalism and coherentism, and the challenges

posed by skepticism shape the discourse within epistemology. The quest for justification, the reliability of belief formation, and the examination of contextual and social dimensions of knowledge further enrich the field. By engaging with the theories and perspectives within epistemology, we deepen our understanding of the complexities of knowledge and the processes through which we attain it. In the following chapters, we will continue our philosophical journey, exploring other branches of philosophy and the enduring questions that captivate human minds.

# Chapter 8 Philosophy of Mind Exploring Consciousness and the Self

Introduction:

The philosophy of mind is a branch of philosophy that examines the nature of consciousness, mental phenomena, and the relationship between the mind and the physical world. In this chapter, we delve into the mysteries of the mind, exploring questions about the nature of consciousness, the self, and the mind-body problem. Through the lens of philosophy of mind, we seek to unravel the complexities of human cognition and subjective experience.

8.1 The Nature of Consciousness:

Consciousness is a central topic within the philosophy of mind. It refers to our subjective awareness of ourselves and the world around us. Philosophers explore the nature of consciousness and attempt to understand its origin, properties, and relationship to the physical brain. Questions such as "What is it like to be conscious?" and "How does consciousness arise?" lie at the heart of this inquiry.

8.2 The Mind-Body Problem:
The mind-body problem is a longstanding philosophical puzzle that examines the relationship between the mind and the physical body. It raises questions about the nature of mental states and their connection to the physical brain. Dualism, as proposed by René Descartes, posits that the mind and body are separate substances, while materialism suggests that mental phenomena are reducible to physical processes. Various perspectives, such as property dualism and identity theory, offer alternative approaches to resolving the mind-body problem.

8.3 Philosophical Behaviorism and Functionalism:
Behaviorism, a psychological theory with philosophical implications, asserts that mental states should be understood solely in terms of observable behavior. Philosophical behaviorism takes this approach further, suggesting that mental states are nothing more than dispositions to behave in certain ways. Functionalism, on the other hand, emphasizes the functional roles of mental states in relation to inputs, outputs, and the overall cognitive system. It focuses on the processes and functions of the mind rather than its specific physical or behavioral manifestations.

8.4 Consciousness and Qualia:
The study of consciousness also encompasses the exploration of qualia, which refers to the subjective qualities of conscious experience. Qualia are the raw, qualitative aspects of our sensations, emotions, and perceptions that cannot be reduced to physical or functional descriptions. The philosophical examination of

qualia seeks to understand the nature of subjective experience and the subjective character of consciousness.

8.5 Personal Identity and the Self:

Philosophy of mind explores questions of personal identity and the nature of the self. It raises inquiries about the continuity of the self over time, the relationship between personal identity and memory, and the notion of the narrative self. Philosophers contemplate the nature of selfhood and the factors that contribute to our sense of personal identity.

8.6 Artificial Intelligence and the Mind:

Advances in artificial intelligence (AI) have brought philosophical questions about the mind to the forefront. The field of AI raises inquiries about the possibility of machine consciousness, the nature of intelligence, and the ethical implications of creating artificial minds. Philosophers examine the implications of AI on our understanding of the mind and the boundaries of consciousness.

8.7 Philosophy of Mind and Cognitive Science:

The philosophy of mind intersects with cognitive science, a multidisciplinary field that explores the nature of cognition and mental processes. Philosophy of mind contributes to cognitive science by addressing philosophical questions about the mind, consciousness, and the nature of mental representations. It engages in dialogue with neuroscience, psychology, linguistics, and artificial intelligence to deepen our understanding of the human mind.

Conclusion:

The philosophy of mind explores the nature of consciousness, the mind-body relationship, and the complexities of human cognition. It grapples with questions about the nature of subjective experience, the self, and the mind's connection to the physical world. The exploration of consciousness, the mind-body problem, and the examination of philosophical perspectives such as behaviorism, functionalism, and qualia shed light on the intricacies of the mind. The philosophy of mind also intersects with the domains of personal identity, artificial intelligence, and cognitive science, further expanding our understanding of the human condition. By engaging with these philosophical inquiries, we gain deeper insights into the nature of consciousness, the self, and the complexities of the mind. In the following chapters, we will continue our philosophical journey, exploring other branches of philosophy and delving further into the profound questions that captivate human thought.

# Chapter 9 Philosophy of Science Exploring the Nature and Methods of Scientific Inquiry

Introduction:

The philosophy of science examines the nature, methods, and limits of scientific inquiry. It investigates the principles that underlie scientific knowledge, the nature of scientific explanation, and the relationship between science and other areas of human understanding. In this chapter, we delve into the philosophy of science, exploring the intricacies of scientific knowledge and the philosophical questions that arise in the practice of scientific inquiry.

9.1 The Scientific Method:

The scientific method is a foundational framework for scientific inquiry. It involves systematic observation, hypothesis formulation, experimentation, data analysis, and the formulation of theories and laws. The philosophy of science investigates the principles and processes that guide scientific investigations, including questions about the reliability of empirical evidence, the role of theory in scientific practice, and the criteria for scientific explanation.

9.2 Scientific Realism and Antirealism:
Scientific realism asserts that scientific theories provide an accurate description of an objective reality that exists independently of human observation. Realists argue that scientific theories aim to uncover the underlying structure and mechanisms of the world. Antirealism, on the other hand, challenges the claim that scientific theories provide a true representation of reality. Antirealists argue that scientific theories are simply useful tools for organizing and predicting observations, without necessarily revealing the ultimate truth.

9.3 Falsification and Confirmation:
Falsification and confirmation are concepts central to the philosophy of science. Falsificationism, proposed by Karl Popper, suggests that scientific theories should be falsifiable, meaning that they can be subjected to tests that could potentially prove them false. Falsification is seen as a crucial criterion for distinguishing between scientific and non-scientific claims. Confirmation, on the other hand, concerns the support and evidence that lend credibility to scientific theories. The problem of induction, raised by David Hume, challenges the logic of using past observations to confirm or support general claims.

9.4 The Structure of Scientific Revolutions:
Thomas Kuhn's work on the structure of scientific revolutions revolutionized the philosophy of science. Kuhn argued that scientific progress occurs through paradigm shifts, where existing theories and frameworks are replaced by new ones. He emphasized the role of scientific communities, social factors, and the influence of

scientific paradigms on the direction of scientific research. Kuhn's ideas sparked discussions about the nature of scientific progress, scientific consensus, and the role of anomalies in scientific revolutions.

9.5 Reductionism and Holism:

Reductionism and holism are contrasting views on the nature of scientific explanation and understanding. Reductionism suggests that complex phenomena can be explained by reducing them to simpler, more fundamental components or laws. It seeks to explain higher-level phenomena in terms of lower-level constituents. Holism, on the other hand, emphasizes the importance of understanding complex systems as wholes, considering the interactions and emergent properties that arise from their components. The debate between reductionism and holism raises questions about the appropriate level of analysis in scientific inquiry.

9.6 Values and Objectivity in Science:

The role of values in science is an ongoing topic of discussion within the philosophy of science. Critics argue that scientific inquiry is not completely objective and is influenced by social, cultural, and personal values. They highlight the potential for bias, value-ladenness in research questions, and the influence of funding and political interests. The examination of values in science explores the interplay between objectivity, values, and the pursuit of knowledge.

9.7 Interdisciplinary Science and the Philosophy of Science:

The philosophy of science also engages with interdisciplinary science, which bridges multiple disciplines to tackle complex problems. Interdisciplinary research raises unique challenges in terms of integrating different methodologies, theories, and perspectives. The philosophy of science contributes to the understanding of interdisciplinary science by examining questions about the nature of disciplinary boundaries, the integration of different knowledge systems, and the potential for fruitful collaborations across disciplines.

Conclusion:

The philosophy of science explores the nature, methods, and challenges of scientific inquiry. It examines the scientific method, the criteria for scientific explanation, and the nature of scientific realism and antirealism. The examination of falsification and confirmation raises questions about the validity and reliability of scientific theories. The exploration of the structure of scientific revolutions, reductionism and holism, and the role of values in science further enrich our understanding of the scientific enterprise. The philosophy of science also intersects with interdisciplinary research, exploring the challenges and potential of integrating different disciplines. By engaging with these philosophical inquiries, we gain deeper insights into the nature of scientific knowledge and the complexities of scientific practice. In the following chapters, we will continue our philosophical journey, exploring other branches of philosophy and delving further into the profound questions that captivate human thought.

# Chapter 10 Ethics of Technology Navigating the Ethical Challenges of a Technological World

Introduction:
The rapid advancement of technology in today's world brings forth a host of ethical challenges and considerations. In this chapter, we delve into the ethics of technology, exploring the moral implications of technological development, the responsible use of technology, and the ethical dilemmas that arise in various technological domains. By examining the ethical dimensions of technology, we aim to navigate the complex landscape of our increasingly technologically driven society.

10.1 Technological Determinism and Ethical Responsibility:
Technological determinism is the perspective that technology shapes and influences society and human behavior. Ethical responsibility arises from the recognition that technology is not neutral but carries ethical implications. We explore the ethical responsibilities of individuals, organizations, and society at large in shaping and deploying technology. This includes considerations of accountability, transparency, and the promotion of ethical

values in technological development.

10.2 Privacy and Data Ethics:
The pervasiveness of technology raises concerns about privacy and the ethical use of data. The collection, storage, and analysis of personal information have become increasingly prevalent. Ethical questions arise regarding the appropriate use of data, the protection of privacy rights, and the potential for misuse or abuse of personal information. We delve into the ethical considerations surrounding data privacy, informed consent, data breaches, and the balance between individual privacy and societal benefits.

10.3 Artificial Intelligence and Ethical Decision-Making:
The development of artificial intelligence (AI) systems raises significant ethical questions. AI systems have the potential to make decisions and take actions that impact individuals and society. Ethical concerns include issues of bias, fairness, accountability, and transparency in AI algorithms. We explore the ethical dimensions of AI, including the responsibility to ensure AI systems align with moral values and principles, and the potential societal impacts of AI technology.

10.4 Digital Ethics and Online Behavior:
The digital realm presents its own set of ethical challenges. Online behavior, including social media use, cyberbullying, and online harassment, raises questions about digital ethics. We examine the ethical implications of digital interactions, the responsible use of social media platforms, and the need for ethical guidelines and responsible online

behavior. The impact of technology on our personal relationships, well-being, and mental health is also considered.

10.5 Technological Impact on Work and Employment:
Technological advancements, such as automation and artificial intelligence, have significant implications for work and employment. Ethical concerns arise in relation to job displacement, the impact on workers' livelihoods, and the potential for inequality. We explore the ethical dimensions of technological impact on work, including considerations of social justice, equitable distribution of benefits, and the responsibility to address the potential negative consequences of technological advancements.

10.6 Environmental Ethics and Sustainable Technology:
The development and use of technology have environmental consequences. Ethical considerations of sustainable technology include minimizing environmental harm, reducing resource consumption, and promoting sustainable practices. We explore the ethical dimensions of environmental impact in technological development, the responsibility of technology companies and individuals to adopt sustainable practices, and the potential for technology to contribute to environmental solutions.

10.7 Global Technological Equity and Access:
Technology has the potential to bridge gaps and provide opportunities, but it also raises questions of equity and access. Ethical considerations include ensuring equitable access to technology and addressing the digital divide, both within and between countries. We explore the ethical

implications of technological inequities, the responsibility to bridge the digital divide, and the promotion of inclusive and equitable technological development.

Conclusion:

The ethics of technology encompass a broad range of ethical challenges and considerations. As technology continues to shape and transform our world, it is crucial to navigate the ethical dimensions of its development and use. Privacy and data ethics, AI and ethical decision-making, digital ethics, the impact on work and employment, sustainable technology, and global technological equity are just a few areas where ethical questions arise. By engaging with these ethical considerations, we can strive for responsible and ethical technological practices that prioritize human well-being, social justice, and sustainability. In the following chapters, we will continue our philosophical journey, exploring other branches of philosophy and delving further into the profound questions that captivate human thought.

# Chapter 11 Aesthetics Exploring the Philosophy of Art and Beauty

Introduction:

Aesthetics is a branch of philosophy that explores the nature, perception, and appreciation of art, beauty, and the aesthetic experience. In this chapter, we delve into the realm of aesthetics, examining philosophical theories and perspectives on the nature of art, the concept of beauty, and the role of aesthetics in human culture. By exploring aesthetics, we aim to deepen our understanding of the profound influence of art and beauty on our lives.

11.1 The Nature of Art:

Aesthetics begins by addressing the fundamental question of what constitutes art. Philosophers explore the defining characteristics of art, the distinction between art and non-art, and the boundaries of artistic expression. Various theories propose different criteria for identifying and defining art, ranging from formalist approaches that emphasize the formal qualities of an artwork to representational theories that focus on the ability of art to depict or express meaning.

11.2 Beauty and Aesthetic Judgment:
Beauty is a central concept within aesthetics. Philosophers contemplate the nature of beauty, seeking to understand its subjective and objective aspects. They explore questions such as "What makes something beautiful?" and "How do we judge aesthetic value?" Aesthetic judgments involve the assessment of beauty, whether in artworks, natural landscapes, or everyday objects. Philosophers examine the criteria and principles that guide aesthetic judgment and the cultural and historical influences on our perception of beauty.

11.3 Theories of Artistic Expression:
Theories of artistic expression delve into the ways in which artists communicate and convey meaning through their works. Interpretation and the relationship between the artist's intention and the viewer's interpretation are key considerations. Expressive theories explore how artworks can evoke emotions, express ideas, or reflect the artist's worldview. The examination of artistic expression involves the analysis of symbols, metaphor, imagery, and the role of context in understanding artistic intent.

11.4 Aesthetic Experience and the Sublime:
Aesthetic experience encompasses the range of emotional and intellectual responses elicited by encounters with art and beauty. The sublime, a concept within aesthetics, refers to the experience of encountering something vast, awe-inspiring, or overwhelming, often accompanied by a sense of both fear and wonder. Philosophers explore the nature of aesthetic experience, the impact of art on our emotions and imagination, and the transformative power

of beauty.

11.5 Aesthetics and Cultural Context:
Aesthetics is deeply embedded in cultural context. Different cultures and historical periods have distinct aesthetic traditions, preferences, and values. Philosophers investigate the influence of culture on aesthetic standards, the role of tradition and innovation in artistic production, and the ways in which cultural context shapes our aesthetic sensibilities. The examination of aesthetics in cultural context sheds light on the diversity and richness of artistic expression across time and societies.

11.6 Ethics and Aesthetics:
The relationship between ethics and aesthetics is a topic of philosophical inquiry. Some argue that beauty and moral value are interconnected, with beauty embodying moral qualities. Others suggest that aesthetics and ethics occupy separate realms, with aesthetics focusing on the sensory and emotional dimensions of experience while ethics addresses moral principles and values. The exploration of the connection between ethics and aesthetics raises questions about the role of art in moral education and the potential ethical implications of aesthetic judgments.

11.7 Aesthetics and Everyday Life:
Aesthetics extends beyond the realm of art to permeate various aspects of everyday life. Philosophers examine the aesthetics of everyday objects, architecture, design, and the built environment. They explore how aesthetics influences our experience of the world and the role of aesthetics in shaping our environments. The examination of aesthetics

in everyday life highlights the pervasive influence of beauty and design on our well-being and quality of life.

Conclusion:

Aesthetics delves into the philosophy of art, beauty, and the aesthetic experience. It explores the nature of art, the concept of beauty, and the ways in which artists express meaning through their works. Aesthetics examines the emotional and intellectual responses evoked by encounters with art, including the experience of the sublime. Cultural context shapes aesthetic sensibilities, while the connection between aesthetics and ethics raises questions about the relationship between beauty and morality. Aesthetics also extends to everyday life, influencing our perception of the world and the design of our environments. By engaging with aesthetics, we deepen our understanding of the profound influence of art and beauty on human culture, creativity, and the human experience. In the following chapters, we will continue our philosophical journey, exploring other branches of philosophy and delving further into the profound questions that captivate human thought.

# Chapter 12 Political Philosophy Examining Power, Justice, and Governance

Introduction:
Political philosophy is a branch of philosophy that explores the nature, origins, and principles of political power, justice, and governance. In this chapter, we delve into the realm of political philosophy, examining different theories and perspectives on the organization of society, the distribution of power, and the principles that guide political institutions. By exploring political philosophy, we aim to deepen our understanding of the foundations of political systems and the pursuit of a just society.

12.1 The State of Nature and Social Contract:
Political philosophy often begins by examining the hypothetical state of nature, a concept that imagines human existence without a governing authority. Philosophers explore the social contract theory, which suggests that individuals voluntarily form a social contract to establish political institutions and give up certain rights in exchange for social order and protection. The social contract provides a theoretical foundation for understanding the legitimacy of political authority.

12.2 Theories of Justice:
Justice is a central concept within political philosophy. Philosophers explore different theories of justice, seeking to establish principles for the fair distribution of resources, opportunities, and rights within society. From utilitarianism, which emphasizes maximizing overall happiness, to theories of distributive justice, which focus on fair allocation of resources, philosophers grapple with the complexities of justice and the pursuit of a just society.

12.3 Forms of Government:
Political philosophy examines various forms of government and their merits and flaws. From democracy, which emphasizes the participation and representation of the people, to monarchy, aristocracy, and oligarchy, philosophers evaluate different systems of governance. They explore questions of power, accountability, and the balance between individual freedoms and collective decision-making.

12.4 Individual Liberty and the Role of the State:
The tension between individual liberty and the authority of the state is a central theme within political philosophy. Philosophers consider the appropriate scope and limits of state power, exploring questions of individual rights, civil liberties, and the role of the state in promoting the common good. They examine the balance between protecting individual freedoms and ensuring the well-being and stability of society.

12.5 Political Legitimacy and Authority:
The concept of political legitimacy addresses the rightful

exercise of political power. Philosophers explore the grounds on which political authority is justified and the conditions under which individuals are obligated to obey the state. They examine theories of legitimacy, including consent-based theories and theories based on the principles of justice and fairness.

12.6 Political Ideologies:
Political philosophy encompasses the examination of different political ideologies, such as liberalism, conservatism, socialism, and anarchism. These ideologies offer distinct perspectives on the role of the state, individual rights, economic systems, and social equality. Philosophers analyze the foundations and implications of these ideologies, exploring their strengths and weaknesses in addressing social and political challenges.

12.7 Global Justice and Cosmopolitanism:
Political philosophy extends beyond the borders of individual states to consider questions of global justice and cosmopolitanism. Philosophers explore the ethical obligations that arise in the global context, addressing issues such as global poverty, human rights, and environmental sustainability. They examine the responsibilities of individuals, states, and the international community in addressing global challenges and promoting justice on a global scale.

Conclusion:
Political philosophy delves into the nature of political power, justice, and governance. It explores theories of the social contract, theories of justice, and different forms of

government. The tension between individual liberty and state authority, questions of political legitimacy and authority, and the examination of political ideologies shape the discourse within political philosophy. The exploration of global justice and cosmopolitanism extends the scope of political philosophy to address ethical obligations in the global context. By engaging with these philosophical inquiries, we deepen our understanding of the foundations of political systems and the pursuit of a just society. In the following chapters, we will continue our philosophical journey, exploring other branches of philosophy and delving further into the profound questions that captivate human thought.

# Chapter 13 Existentialism Embracing Freedom, Authenticity, and the Search for Meaning

Introduction:

Existentialism is a philosophical movement that focuses on the individual's existence, freedom, and the search for meaning in an absurd and uncertain world. In this chapter, we delve into the realm of existentialism, exploring the key concepts and themes that define this philosophical perspective. From the examination of human freedom and responsibility to the exploration of anxiety, authenticity, and the quest for meaning, existentialism offers insights into the human condition and the challenges of living a meaningful life.

13.1 Existential Freedom and Responsibility:

Existentialism places a strong emphasis on human freedom and the responsibility that comes with it. Philosophers explore the idea that individuals are radically free to make choices and shape their own lives, despite the limitations and constraints of existence. Existentialism emphasizes the significance of personal responsibility in determining one's own path and the consequences of choices.

13.2 Authenticity and Inauthenticity:
Authenticity is a core concept in existentialism. It refers to living in accordance with one's true self, values, and convictions. Existentialists argue that individuals often face the temptation to conform to societal expectations, leading to inauthenticity and a loss of personal freedom. The quest for authenticity involves self-reflection, self-acceptance, and the courage to live in alignment with one's genuine desires and beliefs.

13.3 Existential Anxiety and Angst:
Existentialism acknowledges the pervasive presence of existential anxiety and angst in human existence. Philosophers explore the anxiety that arises from the awareness of our mortality, the uncertainty of the future, and the responsibility of creating meaning in a world without inherent meaning. Existential anxiety highlights the challenges and struggles individuals face in navigating the complexities of life.

13.4 Absurdity and the Absurd Condition:
Existentialism confronts the notion of the absurd, which refers to the inherent lack of rational meaning or purpose in the universe. Existentialists argue that individuals must confront the absurd condition of existence and create their own meaning in the face of this existential void. They explore the tension between the human desire for meaning and the recognition of life's inherent absurdity.

13.5 Existentialism and the Search for Meaning:
Existentialism offers insights into the search for meaning in life. Philosophers delve into questions of purpose,

values, and the quest for a meaningful existence. Existentialism suggests that meaning is not pre-determined but is a product of personal choice, commitment, and engagement with the world. The search for meaning involves the exploration of personal values, the pursuit of authentic goals, and the cultivation of meaningful relationships.

13.6 Existentialism and Existential Therapy:
Existentialism has applications beyond philosophy, particularly in the field of psychotherapy. Existential therapy focuses on the individual's experience of existence, freedom, and the search for meaning. It encourages individuals to confront existential challenges, make choices aligned with their values, and take responsibility for their lives. Existential therapy emphasizes the importance of personal agency and self-reflection in fostering psychological well-being.

13.7 Existentialism and Social and Political Dimensions:
Existentialism also engages with social and political dimensions. Existentialists explore questions of authenticity and freedom within societal structures, the impact of social and cultural forces on individual existence, and the responsibility of individuals to engage in the social and political sphere. They challenge oppressive systems and advocate for personal freedom, social justice, and the recognition of individual dignity.

Conclusion:
Existentialism provides a philosophical lens through which we can understand the complexities of human existence. It

highlights the significance of individual freedom, responsibility, and authenticity in shaping a meaningful life. Existentialism acknowledges the challenges of living in an absurd and uncertain world and invites individuals to confront existential anxiety and embrace personal agency. The search for meaning becomes a personal journey of self-discovery, reflection, and the pursuit of authentic values. Existentialism also offers insights into the realms of psychotherapy, social justice, and political engagement. By engaging with existentialist concepts, we deepen our understanding of the human condition and the potential for self-actualization and personal growth. In the following chapters, we will continue our philosophical journey, exploring other branches of philosophy and delving further into the profound questions that captivate human thought.

# Chapter 14 Feminist Philosophy Challenging Patriarchy and Promoting Gender Equality

Introduction:

Feminist philosophy is a branch of philosophy that critically examines the social, political, and cultural structures that perpetuate gender inequality and oppression. In this chapter, we delve into the realm of feminist philosophy, exploring key concepts, theories, and perspectives that challenge patriarchal norms and advocate for gender equality. From the analysis of power dynamics and intersectionality to the exploration of feminist ethics and the politics of identity, feminist philosophy offers insights into the struggle for gender justice and the pursuit of a more equitable society.

14.1 Gender and Social Construction:

Feminist philosophy challenges the notion that gender is a fixed and natural category. It examines how gender is socially constructed and shaped by cultural norms and expectations. Philosophers explore the ways in which gender roles, stereotypes, and expectations are perpetuated and reinforced in society. The analysis of gender as a social construct highlights the fluidity and diversity of gender identities and experiences.

14.2 Patriarchy and Power:
Feminist philosophy critiques patriarchal systems and power structures that perpetuate gender inequality. Philosophers examine the ways in which patriarchy operates, shaping social institutions, norms, and power dynamics. They analyze the unequal distribution of power between genders and explore strategies for challenging patriarchal hierarchies and creating more egalitarian societies.

14.3 Intersectionality and Multiple Oppressions:
Intersectionality is a central concept in feminist philosophy, highlighting the interconnected nature of various forms of oppression. Philosophers explore how gender intersects with other social categories such as race, class, sexuality, and disability. They examine how intersecting oppressions create unique experiences and challenges for individuals and advocate for an inclusive feminism that recognizes and addresses multiple forms of oppression.

14.4 Feminist Ethics:
Feminist philosophy offers a critique of traditional ethical theories that often overlook or marginalize women's experiences and perspectives. Feminist ethicists explore the ethics of care, relationality, and the importance of context in moral decision-making. They emphasize the significance of empathy, compassion, and interconnectedness in ethical deliberation and challenge the prioritization of abstract principles over lived experiences.

14.5 Gender and Language:
Feminist philosophy examines the ways in which language reflects and reinforces gender norms and inequalities. Philosophers analyze the use of gendered language, the impact of language on identity formation, and the potential for language to perpetuate stereotypes and exclusion. They explore inclusive language practices and the role of language in challenging gender biases and promoting gender equality.

14.6 Feminism and the Politics of Identity:
Feminist philosophy engages with the politics of identity, recognizing the diverse experiences and perspectives of individuals within feminist movements. Philosophers explore the tensions and debates surrounding issues of intersectionality, solidarity, and inclusivity within feminist activism. They examine the ways in which feminist movements have evolved and adapted to address the complexities of gender inequality in different contexts.

14.7 Feminism and Social Change:
Feminist philosophy is concerned with social and political transformation to achieve gender justice. Philosophers explore strategies for feminist activism, advocacy, and social change. They examine the role of grassroots movements, policy reform, and cultural shifts in challenging gender inequality and creating more equitable societies. They also critically assess the potential limitations and challenges of feminist movements in achieving lasting social change.

Conclusion:

Feminist philosophy critically examines the structures of power, inequality, and oppression that perpetuate gender inequality. It challenges traditional notions of gender, analyzes the dynamics of patriarchy, and advocates for gender equality. Intersectionality and the recognition of multiple forms of oppression shape feminist analysis, highlighting the interconnectedness of social categories. Feminist ethics emphasize care, relationality, and the importance of context in moral decision-making. Language and identity are also central concerns, as feminist philosophy explores the impact of language on gender norms and the politics of identity within feminist movements. Ultimately, feminist philosophy strives for social change, advocating for a more just and equitable society. By engaging with feminist concepts and theories, we deepen our understanding of the complexities of gender inequality and the potential for transformative social action. In the following chapters, we will continue our philosophical journey, exploring other branches of philosophy and delving further into the profound questions that captivate human thought.

# Chapter 15 Environmental Philosophy Exploring Humanity's Relationship with Nature and the Environment

Introduction:
Environmental philosophy is a branch of philosophy that explores the ethical, metaphysical, and epistemological dimensions of humanity's relationship with the natural world. In this chapter, we delve into the realm of environmental philosophy, examining key concepts, theories, and perspectives that address the environmental challenges we face today. From the examination of our ethical responsibilities towards nature to the exploration of environmental justice and sustainability, environmental philosophy offers insights into our interconnectedness with the environment and the need for a harmonious coexistence with the natural world.

15.1 Anthropocentrism vs. Ecocentrism:
Environmental philosophy explores different approaches to understanding humanity's place in the natural world. Anthropocentrism places human beings at the center of ethical consideration, prioritizing human interests and well-being. In contrast, ecocentrism recognizes the intrinsic value of all living beings and ecosystems, emphasizing the interconnectedness and interdependence of the natural

world. Philosophers examine the ethical implications of these perspectives and advocate for a more ecocentric worldview.

15.2 Ethics and Environmental Responsibility:
Ethics plays a central role in environmental philosophy. Philosophers explore ethical theories and frameworks that guide our responsibilities towards nature. Environmental ethics examines questions of moral considerability, the rights of non-human beings, and the moral implications of human actions on the environment. It also delves into the intergenerational ethics of sustainability, recognizing the importance of preserving the environment for future generations.

15.3 Deep Ecology and Biocentrism:
Deep ecology is a perspective within environmental philosophy that emphasizes the intrinsic value of all living beings and ecosystems. It promotes a holistic view of nature and advocates for a radical shift in human attitudes and behaviors towards the environment. Biocentrism, a related concept, argues for the inherent worth and dignity of all living beings, not just human beings. Deep ecology and biocentrism challenge anthropocentric perspectives and call for a reevaluation of our relationship with the natural world.

15.4 Environmental Justice and Equity:
Environmental philosophy addresses the social and environmental injustices that disproportionately affect marginalized communities. Philosophers explore the intersection between social justice and environmental

concerns, examining the unequal distribution of environmental burdens and benefits. They advocate for environmental justice, which seeks to ensure fair access to a clean and healthy environment, and recognize the importance of inclusivity and equity in environmental decision-making.

15.5 Sustainability and the Ethics of Stewardship:
Sustainability is a critical concept within environmental philosophy, highlighting the need to live in harmony with nature and preserve the Earth's resources for future generations. Philosophers explore the ethics of stewardship, which emphasizes our responsibility to care for and protect the environment. They examine sustainable practices, the challenges of balancing human needs with ecological limits, and the role of technology and innovation in achieving sustainability.

15.6 Environmental Aesthetics:
Environmental philosophy also engages with the aesthetic dimensions of our relationship with nature. Philosophers explore the aesthetic appreciation of the natural world, the value of beauty in environmental preservation, and the role of art and literature in fostering a deeper connection with nature. They examine the ways in which aesthetic experiences in nature contribute to our understanding and appreciation of the environment.

15.7 Ecofeminism and the Intersection of Gender and the Environment:
Ecofeminism is a perspective within environmental philosophy that explores the intersection of gender and the

environment. It examines the ways in which patriarchal structures and the domination of nature are intertwined, highlighting the importance of gender equality and environmental sustainability. Ecofeminists advocate for a reevaluation of hierarchical and oppressive systems and promote the empowerment of women and the protection of nature.

Conclusion:

Environmental philosophy delves into humanity's relationship with nature and the environment. It explores ethical responsibilities towards nature, addressing anthropocentrism, and advocating for ecocentric perspectives. Environmental justice emphasizes the need for equitable distribution of environmental resources and the recognition of the rights of marginalized communities. Sustainability calls for responsible stewardship of the environment and the promotion of practices that ensure the well-being of future generations. The aesthetic appreciation of nature fosters a deeper connection with the environment, while ecofeminism highlights the intersection of gender and the environment. By engaging with environmental philosophy, we deepen our understanding of our interconnectedness with nature and the importance of living in harmony with the environment. In the following chapters, we will continue our philosophical journey, exploring other branches of philosophy and delving further into the profound questions that captivate human thought.

# Conclusion

"Reflections of the Mind: Exploring Philosophy's Depths" has been a profound journey through the vast landscape of philosophy, delving into the depths of human thought and illuminating the fundamental questions that shape our understanding of the world and ourselves. Throughout this exploration, we have encountered diverse perspectives, engaged in thought-provoking discussions, and embraced the complexities of existence.

As we reach the conclusion of this book, it is crucial to recognize the transformative power of philosophy. It has challenged our assumptions, broadened our perspectives, and cultivated critical thinking skills. Philosophy serves as a beacon of intellectual curiosity, inviting us to question, explore, and seek wisdom in the pursuit of truth and meaning.

The journey of "Reflections of the Mind" has provided insights into metaphysics, epistemology, ethics, aesthetics, political philosophy, existentialism, feminist philosophy, and environmental philosophy. We have grappled with the nature of reality, the sources of knowledge, the foundations of morality, and the complexities of the human experience. Each chapter has offered a unique lens through which we have examined these profound questions, gaining a deeper understanding of ourselves and our place in the world.

Throughout this exploration, we have discovered that philosophy is not merely an academic pursuit but a guide to living a more examined and meaningful life. It encourages us to embrace complexity, to challenge dogma, and to cultivate empathy and compassion. Philosophy fosters intellectual humility, recognizing that there are no easy answers, but rather a continuous process of questioning and refining our understanding.

As we conclude this journey, it is important to carry the lessons learned from philosophy into our daily lives. Let us remain open to new ideas, engage in thoughtful dialogue, and continue to ask the difficult questions that challenge our assumptions. May philosophy be a source of inspiration, a tool for personal growth, and a guide for navigating the complexities of existence.

"Reflections of the Mind" has invited us to embark on an intellectual adventure, expanding our horizons and deepening our insights. Let us carry the wisdom and transformative power of philosophy with us, as we navigate the intricate tapestry of life, driven by curiosity, guided by reason, and grounded in the pursuit of truth and understanding.

Thank you for joining us on this remarkable journey through the depths of philosophy. May the reflections within these pages continue to inspire, challenge, and empower you as you embark on your own path of intellectual exploration and personal growth.

With heartfelt gratitude and profound admiration,[Author's Name]

9 789358 830514